SCIENCE SLEUTHS

The Case of the Smelly Water

By Glen Phelan

Illustrated by C.B. Canga

PICTURE CREDITS
45 (top to bottom) © Swerve/Alamy, © Anna
Clopet/Corbis; 46 (top to bottom) © Jonathan
Blair/Corbis, © Rosemary Greenwood;
Ecoscene/Corbis; 48 © Mark Edwards/Still
Pictures/Peter Arnold, Inc.

Produced through the worldwide resources of
the National Geographic Society, John M. Fahey,
Jr., President and Chief Executive Officer;
Gilbert M. Grosvenor, Chairman of the Board;
Nina D. Hoffman, Executive Vice President and
President, Books and Education Publishing
Group.

**PREPARED BY NATIONAL GEOGRAPHIC
SCHOOL PUBLISHING**
Ericka Markman, Senior Vice President and
President, Children's Books and Education
Publishing Group; Steve Mico, Senior Vice
President, Publisher, Editorial Director; Francis
Downey, Executive Editor; Richard Easby,
Editorial Manager; Bea Jackson, Director of
Design; Cynthia Olson, Art Director; Margaret
Sidlosky, Director of Illustrations; Matt
Wascavage, Manager of Publishing Services;
Lisa Pergolizzi, Sean Philpotts, Production
Managers, Ted Tucker, Production Specialist.

MANUFACTURING AND QUALITY CONTROL
Christopher A. Liedel, Chief Financial Officer;
Phillip L. Schlosser, Director; Clifton M.
Brown, Manager.

EDITORS
Barbara Seeber, Mary Anne Wengel

BOOK DEVELOPMENT
Morrison BookWorks LLC

BOOK DESIGN
Steven Curtis Design

ART DIRECTION
Dan Banks, Project Design Company

Published by the National Geographic Society
1145 17th Street, N.W.
Washington, D.C. 20036-4688

ISBN: 0-7922-5851-7

2010 2009
 2 3 4 5 6 7 8 9 10 11 12 13 14 15

Printed in U.S.A.

Contents

Meet the Science Sleuths

Jamie

Jamie loves drawing and photography. She is a good observer.

Marco

Marco enjoys doing research. He wants to know how things work.

Vanessa

Vanessa is adventurous. She is good at doing science experiments.

Kyle

Kyle likes to interview people. He wants to be a reporter someday.

What's in the Water?

"Just one more to go," said Madison Harold. As she knelt, she used a trowel to dig a small hole in the ground. She carefully set the plant in the hole and filled it with soil. Then she pressed down on the soil so the young plant would stay in place.

Madison leaned back. She and her dad admired the three rows of geraniums they had just planted.

"OK," said her dad. "Let's give them a drink."

"Oh, let me!" Madison scrambled to her feet. She picked up the hose and turned the nozzle. A spray of water shot out.

The water looked so refreshing. Madison couldn't resist taking a drink. She put her lips to the stream of water.

"Yuck!"

"What is it, Maddy?"

"This water tastes terrible," Madison said as she made a face. "It smells funny too."

"Maybe there was some dirt on the tip of the nozzle and it got in the water."

Madison looked at the nozzle. "No, the water was running for a while before I took a drink. It should be clean," she said.

"Maybe there was something in the hose," offered her dad.

That didn't sound right either. But Madison didn't think much about it. She just shrugged her shoulders. "Well, I hope the flowers like it better than I do."

Madison finished watering the plants. Then she rinsed all the mud off her hands. She was sweating, and the cold water felt good. But she never did get her drink.

"I'm going to get a drink inside," she said. She went to the kitchen and turned on the faucet. She peered at the stream of water. It was as clear as ever. She poured herself a glass. She took a big gulp. "Oh, yuck!" she said again. It tasted just like the water from the hose.

She sniffed the glass of water. It had a musty smell. It reminded her of the water in her aquarium when it hadn't been cleaned for a while. She poured it into the sink and reached for the bottled water in the refrigerator instead.

Just then Mr. Harold came in. "Dad, taste the water. It's just like it was outside."

He half-filled a glass from the faucet and took a sip. "Yeah, I see what you mean. And it smells bad too. Looks fine though," he said holding it up to the window.

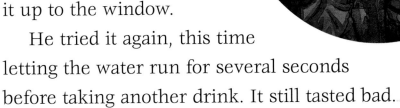

He tried it again, this time letting the water run for several seconds before taking another drink. It still tasted bad.

"Do you think it's safe for us to drink?" asked Madison.

"I think we would have heard something on the news if the water was unsafe."

"Well, it still stinks," said Madison. She thought for a moment. "Where does our water come from anyway?"

"It comes from the lake."

Madison and her family lived near a lake, not too far from Rochester, New York.

"This is so strange," said Madison, frowning. "The water tasted just fine yesterday. I wonder what's going on."

Madison thought for a moment. Then, she snapped her fingers. "I know what to do! I'll ask the Science Sleuths for help!"

Kyle picked up Jamie's hairbrush from the couch. He tapped it on the table. "I now call this meeting of the Science Sleuths to order," he said in a phony grown-up voice.

Vanessa and Marco laughed. Jamie reached across the table and grabbed the hairbrush. "Give me that," she giggled.

It was Saturday afternoon at Jamie's house. That could only mean one thing—another Science Sleuths meeting.

Jamie had started the club. She lives with her Aunt Jessica and Uncle Bill in Washington, D.C. Aunt Jessica is an editor for a kid's magazine called *National Geographic Explorer!* It has a lot of cool articles on science. Jamie and her friends love reading it. Jamie especially loves the amazing pictures.

One day, Aunt Jessica asked Jamie if she wanted to help with the magazine. She could write articles to answer questions from readers. Jamie jumped at the chance. She asked if her friends could join her. That was the beginning of the Science Sleuths.

The Sleuths met on Saturdays. That's when they reviewed some of the more interesting questions that readers sent in during the week. Most of the questions could be answered by

doing simple research. But some questions were more mysterious. They required some real sleuthing. Those are the ones the Science Sleuths always liked best.

"All right, let's get to work," said Vanessa. "Marco, how do the e-mails look?"

Marco turned toward the computer screen. "We have a few questions here that could be fun to investigate." He started to open the saved e-mails so they could choose the best one. Suddenly another e-mail arrived.

"Whoops, here's one more. Let's open it and see what it says."

Marco read the e-mail aloud. It was from Madison Harold. She explained that her water tasted awful. She said she had checked with her neighbors, and they had the same problem. She wanted to know if the Science Sleuths could help her figure out the mystery.

Looking for Clues

The Sleuths started discussing Madison's problem. "I wonder if there's something wrong with the lake water," said Jamie. "Maybe it's **polluted.**"

"Yeah, but would that happen all of a sudden?" asked Kyle.

"It's possible," replied Jamie. "Let's check the Internet for articles about the lake. Maybe something new is polluting it."

"I'm sure the drinking water doesn't come straight from the lake," said Vanessa. "I think it's cleaned first at a water treatment plant near the lake. We could contact the plant and see if they've noticed any problems."

"Why don't we ask Madison if she can go to the lake to look for clues?" Marco said.

---

pollute – to make dirty or fill with waste

"Like what?" asked Vanessa.

"I don't know. Maybe she'll find pollution, or something else. If this is a brand-new problem, she might see something that hasn't been reported in the news yet."

Kyle shrugged. "That makes sense to me. So what do you guys think? Do we have our next case to solve for the magazine?"

Everyone nodded. They would have to run it by Aunt Jessica, however. She had the final say, but they all thought she would agree.

Marco turned to the computer. "I'll e-mail Madison to tell her we're on the case. And I'll see if she can check out the lake."

"Hey, Mom! Dad!" Madison came running into the family room. She had a sheet of paper in her hand. "Can we go to the lake tomorrow?"

She showed them the printout of the e-mail she had sent and Marco's reply. Her parents agreed that a picnic by the lake would be a fun way to spend a Sunday afternoon.

Madison and her family set out for the lake around noon on Sunday. There was a gentle breeze blowing as Madison helped her parents set up the picnic table. They were in a park on the shore of the lake. The grassy picnic area was next to a small sandy beach. People were splashing and swimming in the cool water.

Nearby was a place where you could rent canoes. Madison's dad had an idea. "What do you say we take a canoe trip after lunch? Then we could explore some of the shoreline."

An hour later, the Harold family was gliding across the lake. They stayed close to the shore because the water was choppy.

Mrs. Harold turned toward Madison. "So Maddy, what are we supposed to be looking for?"

"I don't know. Just anything unusual, I guess. Maybe some kind of pollution."

Mr. Harold looked down into the water. "Well, I don't see any pollution here. In fact, I don't remember the water ever being this clear. I can see right down to the bottom of the lake. And it's about 20 feet deep here."

Madison grabbed the edge of the canoe and leaned over to look. The canoe started tilting.

"Maddy, sit straight," her dad said quickly. The canoe tilted back. "You can't lean that much in a canoe, honey. Just tilt your head and shoulders, not your whole body."

For the next 15 minutes, Madison peered through the clear water. The bottom was mostly sand and smooth rocks. Sometimes they would

pass over an area of green, grassy plants growing on the bottom. Every now and then, she saw a fish. "It seems like there should be more fish swimming around," she said.

They paddled on. The water sparkled in the sunlight while the family enjoyed a breeze. Madison looked ahead and squinted. She pointed to something on the water. "What's that?"

Her mom shielded her eyes from the sun. "Looks like pond scum," she said. "And we're headed right for it."

"Yuck! What's pond scum?"

"**Algae,**" replied her dad. "They look like tiny green plants floating on the water, but they're not really plants."

A few seconds later, the canoe started slicing through the algae. They tried to paddle smoothly so they wouldn't splash it on their clothes. It was a small patch—about the size of their canoe. They passed only a couple other patches of algae as they paddled through the lake.

----

algae – tiny organisms that live in water

"Well, I haven't seen anything that I would call pollution," said Mr. Harold. "No oil slicks. No sewer water being dumped into the lake. I think we'd better turn back."

"Wait. What's that big building up there?" Madison pointed to a building on the shore about half a mile away. "Is it a factory?"

"I think that's the water treatment plant," said her dad. "That's where the lake water gets cleaned. Then underground pipes carry the water from the water plant to the houses in town, right to our faucets."

"Can we go see it?" asked Madison.

"No, it's too far away. We need to get back. Besides, there's no place to leave the canoe."

"But they might be able to tell us what's wrong with the water," Madison said.

"You may be right, Maddy," said her mom. "But we can call them during the week."

That made sense. They turned around and headed back. This time they went around the patch of algae. Madison asked, "Is there always algae in the lake?"

"In the summertime, yes," said her dad. "But I think there's usually more than this on the surface." Madison wondered about that. She wondered if the algae have something to do with the water's taste.

Everyone was barefoot as they stepped out of the canoe and pulled it onto the sandy shore. "Ouch!" said Madison suddenly. She lifted her foot. She had stepped on something sharp.

"Are you all right, Maddy?" her mom asked.

"Yeah, it didn't cut me."

Her dad bent over to see what she had stepped on. He picked it up. It was a small shell. It was white with brown stripes. "Huh, I've never seen one like this," he said. "It looks like some kind of a clam."

They looked around and found several others. Madison thought they were pretty. She picked up a few to take home.

A Key Discovery

That evening, Madison e-mailed the Sleuths about her trip to the lake. She told them how crystal clear the water was, and how there were fewer algae and fish than usual. She described the little shells she found on the shore.

"But we didn't see anything that looked like pollution," Madison wrote in her e-mail. "We explored only a little bit of the lake, though. So there might be pollution somewhere else. We also saw the water treatment plant. But we didn't go there. My mom says we can call the plant during the week. What do you think? Did I miss any clues?"

Jamie finished reading aloud. She had called the rest of the Sleuths over to her house when the e-mail arrived.

"Maybe fewer fish and algae have something to do with pollution," said Kyle.

"But Madison said that the water was very clear," said Marco. "That doesn't sound like pollution to me. By the way, in my research, I didn't find any articles about pollution in the lake."

Vanessa noticed that Jamie was drawing something. "What are you doing, Jamie?" she asked. She peeked over Jamie's shoulder.

"I'm drawing the shell that Madison described in her e-mail."

She held up the finished drawing. "I figured we could find out what kind of shell it is. There's a guidebook on shells at the library."

Just then Aunt Jessica walked down the stairs into Sleuth Headquarters. "Hi, kids. How's the investigation going?" She had already agreed that Madison's smelly water problem was a good one to explore for the magazine.

Jamie showed her Madison's latest e-mail. Then she showed her the drawing. "Hmm. That's odd."

"What's odd?" asked Jamie. The Sleuths all looked at Aunt Jessica.

"Your uncle and I have a friend who spends the summer at a fishing lake in Virginia," Aunt Jessica explained. "He was telling us about some shells he found along the shore. He said they were white with brown stripes, just like this." She pointed to the drawing.

"He was complaining about fewer fish this year. He noticed how clear the water was, too."

The Sleuths were trying to connect clues. "Did he say anything about how the water tasted?" asked Vanessa.

"No, he doesn't drink water from the lake. He has a well at his cabin."

"I wonder if this little shellfish, the clear water, and fewer fish are connected in some way," said Kyle.

"It seems like it," said Vanessa. "But how? And are those shellfish connected to the bad-tasting water?"

"I don't know, but I bet the people at the water treatment plant would," said Kyle.

"I'd really like to see how a water treatment plant works," said Marco.

"Yeah, if we knew that, it might help us to figure out what's wrong with the water," said Jamie.

Aunt Jessica had a great idea. "Why don't we visit one of the treatment plants in the Washington, D.C., area? I think they give tours. We could go tomorrow morning."

"That would be perfect!" said Marco. "But let's check the Internet, too."

Marco found a lot of sites on water treatment plants. The Sleuths saw that water from lakes and rivers goes through the same general steps. Diagrams made it look pretty simple. First, the

water passes through screens that block large items like fish, sticks, and stones. Then the water is mixed with a chemical that turns dirt into little globs. The globs sink to the bottom of a settling tank. Next, the water seeps through a filter of gravel, sand, or other material to remove tiny bits of dirt. Finally, chlorine is added to kill germs. The water comes out clean and ready to drink.

One of the steps didn't make much sense to Kyle. "Does the water really get clean by moving through gravel and sand?" he wondered. "It seems to me it would get dirtier."

"Why don't we do an experiment?" suggested Vanessa. "We can make our own filter and see if it cleans dirty water. Jamie, do you have sand?"

"I have some from my sand art kit. How much do we need?"

"About a cupful should do it. Marco, can you get a handful of gravel from the backyard? Now we need something to put it all in. Jamie, do you have an empty plastic soda bottle?"

"We have one in the recycling bin," said Aunt Jessica. "I'll go get it."

"Great. Could you cut off the bottom?"

"What can I do?" asked Kyle.

"You get the best job of all," replied Vanessa. "You get to make some dirty water."

"Cool!" He darted upstairs.

"OK, we just need some cotton balls and then we're all set," thought Vanessa out loud.

Ten minutes later, everyone was gathered around the homemade water filter. Kyle poured a cup of dirty water into the bottle of sand, gravel, and cotton balls. "That looks disgusting, Kyle," said Vanessa. "What did you put in there?"

"Oh, just a little dirt, pepper, and oil. Oh yeah—and some ketchup. Mmm, mmm!"

"Yuck!"

The dirty water slowly trickled through the sand, gravel, and cotton balls. After about 20 seconds, the water started dripping from the bottle into the cup beneath. It wasn't totally clean, but it was a lot cleaner than before.

"Well, I wouldn't want to drink that water," said Marco, "but it's definitely cleaner than I thought it would be."

"It is," said Jamie. "And a water treatment plant does a much better job than this."

"Then whatever is causing the bad-tasting water must be getting through the filters," inferred Kyle. "I'll have to ask somebody at the water treatment plant about that."

On Monday morning, the Sleuths piled into Aunt Jessica's van and buckled up. "So where are we going, Aunt Jess?" Jamie asked.

"There's a water treatment plant on a lake about an hour north of here. It provides some of the water for the Washington, D.C., area." They headed north into Maryland.

"Welcome, everyone. My name is Paul. I'm an engineer here at the water treatment plant. Today I'll be showing you how we turn this . . . into this." He held up a jar of dirty, greenish water and then a jar of crystal clear water.

The Sleuths' tour group included kids from a summer day camp. Everyone was amazed at the size of the building. Once they went inside, they saw why it was so big. There were huge tanks of water. Some tanks were for mixing the water with chemicals. Some tanks held dirt that had settled out of the water. Water trickled through filters in other tanks.

The Sleuths were glad that they had learned a little about water treatment the night before. It was fun comparing the diagrams from the Web sites with the real thing. Everyone asked lots of

questions. At the end of the tour, one of the day campers asked, "Do any fish get in the water?"

Paul smiled. "No. Remember at the beginning of the tour, I showed you those screens? They block fish from getting into the intake pipe. That's the pipe that brings water from the lake into the treatment plant."

"But there's one critter that's been finding its way into the pipes at some treatment plants. And it's causing a lot of trouble." He reached into his pocket and pulled out a small object. It was a shell—white with brown stripes.

A Very Special Mussel

The same morning that the Sleuths visited the water treatment plant, Madison's mother was on the phone. She was talking to Amanda, an engineer at their water treatment plant. She had just finished telling the engineer about the musty water. Mrs. Harold was holding the phone so Madison could hear too.

"We were on the lake yesterday and we didn't notice any pollution," Mrs. Harold said. "Is there a problem at the treatment plant?"

"No, everything is working fine," said Amanda. "But many people have called to complain about the water. We think that the smell and taste problems might be from algae. There has been more algae than usual this summer."

Mrs. Harold frowned. "But it looked like there was less algae on the lake yesterday."

"Oh yes, there's less algae *on* the lake," Amanda said. "But the algae at the bottom of the lake has increased.

"Chemicals in this type of algae give the water a musty taste. But don't worry, it's safe to drink."

"OK, thanks for the information," Mrs. Harold said. "Oh, by the way, we also found some shells at the beach that I haven't seen before. They are small and white with brown stripes. Do you know what they are?"

"Yes, I do," said Amanda. "And they're a big part of the problem." Mrs. Harold and Madison listened closely.

At that very moment, 300 miles away, the Sleuths were also listening to a plant engineer. Paul held up the shell. "Does anyone know what kind of shell this is?" he asked.

No one did. Jamie had not yet had a chance to go to the library and identify the shell.

"It's called a zebra mussel," Paul continued. "A mussel is a kind of shellfish, like a clam. This mussel has stripes, like a zebra."

"It's pretty," said one of the day campers.

"Yes, it is," agreed Paul. "But it's a real pest."

Kyle recognized the shell. "What kind of trouble does it cause?" he asked.

Paul explained. "The main problem for water treatment plants is that it clogs the intake pipes. The mussels attach to hard surfaces, like the insides of pipes. They attach to each other, too. Thousands of them can build up inside of the intake pipe and block the flow of water."

"Is there a way for the plants to get rid of them?" asked Vanessa.

"At some plants, people have to scrape them out of the pipe. But they keep coming back, so you have to keep scraping. Another way is to have little streams of **chlorine** flow around the

---

chlorine – a disinfecting agent used to purify

opening of the pipe. Remember on the tour, we showed you how we add chlorine to the water to kill bacteria? Well, zebra mussels don't like chlorine either. Chlorine keeps them away from the pipe."

The Sleuths now knew that zebra mussels were in Madison's lake. So Marco asked, "Do zebra mussels make the water taste bad?"

Paul looked surprised. "Yes, they do. But it's not the mussels themselves. The zebra mussels are eating the algae that live on the surface of the lakes. This makes the water clearer. It allows the sun to shine down to the bottom of the lake. This makes the algae on the bottom increase. Has anyone ever seen algae growing under the water?"

Many people raised their hands, including the Sleuths.

"Good. Like every living thing, algae eventually die. When the algae on the bottom of the lake die, they give the water a bad smell and taste. There was less of it before, so when it died, you didn't notice the taste. The water is safe to drink after it goes through a treatment plant, but it still tastes a bit musty."

Kyle had one more question. "Are there zebra mussels in the lake where we are?"

"Not yet," replied Paul. "But they may be working their way here."

Paul could see that everyone looked puzzled, so he explained. "Zebra mussels don't belong in North America. They come from lakes in Eastern Europe. In 1986, some zebra mussels hitched a ride on a ship in its ballast water."

"What's ballast water?" asked Marco.

"That's water that ships suck into huge tanks. The weight of the water tanks keeps the ship from tilting. When the ship gets to another port, it often dumps its ballast water in that port."

"Oh, I get it," said Vanessa. "The mussels were in the water that was sucked into the tanks in the ship. Then they were dumped out with the water in the other port."

"Exactly," said Paul. "And that other port was on the Great Lakes. Since then, zebra mussels have spread to lakes and rivers. They are in many states in the eastern half of the country, but they're not in Maryland yet. And we'd like to keep it that way."

"How can we stop them?" asked Jamie.

"There are many things people can do . . . "

Meanwhile, farther north, Madison and Mrs. Harold were learning more about zebra mussels. Amanda had told them much of the same things that Paul was telling the Sleuths. Then Madison said to her mother, "Ask her how the zebra mussels got to this lake."

Mrs. Harold relayed the question. Amanda replied, "Some mussels were probably attached to the bottom of a boat from another lake or river. In that way, zebra mussels hitchhike from one body of water to another. Besides affecting the taste of water, zebra mussels cause other problems. Did you notice how clean the water looked?"

"Yes. We were wondering about that. But why is that a problem?" asked Mrs. Harold.

"Zebra mussels are big eaters," Amanda said. "They eat by filtering water through their bodies and trapping all the **microscopic** creatures that live in the water. That makes the water clearer, but it leaves less food for fish. So after a while, there are fewer fish."

"We noticed that too," said Mrs. Harold.

"The problem is that an animal that comes from another place usually doesn't have any natural enemies. If the animals who usually prey on the invader aren't there, then the population of the invader goes way up. So an animal, like the zebra mussel, spreads quickly. This can be a disaster for other animals that live there."

Madison understood how all the things she had seen at the lake were connected. She decided to send an e-mail to the Science Sleuths.

microscopic – so small that it cannot be seen without a microscope

The Invaders

By the time the Science Sleuths got back to Jamie's house, there was an e-mail waiting from Madison. She told them everything Amanda had said about the zebra mussels. The Sleuths replied with their own information from Paul. Everyone now had a clear picture of the problem. The zebra mussel was an invader!

"So, how are we going to tell our readers about The Case of the Smelly Water?" Aunt Jessica asked the Sleuths.

It was one of those times when everyone wished they could add a few more pages to the *National Geographic Explorer!* magazine. There was so much to show and tell.

"We have to tell how Madison noticed the taste problem in the first place," said Vanessa.

"Vanessa, don't forget your experiment," said Aunt Jessica. "Our readers would probably like to make a filter to see how a water treatment plant works."

"We should include some quotes from Paul and Amanda—the two water treatment engineers," added Marco. "Kyle, you have notes from the tour, right?"

"Of course I do," said Kyle proudly. He flipped open his notebook. "A good reporter always has good notes."

"We should include the list of things that Paul said people could do to stop zebra mussels from spreading. I have them written down here."

Ways to stop the spread of zebra mussels:

1. Know what a zebra mussel looks like.
2. Report sightings of zebra mussels to the local department of natural resources.
3. Check your boat and trailer for zebra mussels.

Jamie had a good idea. "Why don't we do a couple mini articles about other animal and plant invaders? We could write about the purple loosestrife."

"Purple what?" asked Kyle.

"Purple loosestrife," repeated Jamie. "It's a wildflower." Jamie loved wildflowers and knew a lot about them. "It was brought over from Europe to use in gardens because it's so pretty. But its seeds spread quickly. Now it crowds out other plants that usually grow here."

The Sleuths agreed that it was important to tell their readers about other invaders besides zebra mussels. So they went to the library to do more research. They learned more than they expected.

One invader they learned about was the Burmese python. They found out how this kind of snake was brought from Asia to Florida to be sold as pets. But sometimes the pythons escaped. Or they got to be too much for the owners to handle. Some people released them into the Florida Everglades—the huge marshy land in southern Florida. Now the snakes are a big problem. They gobble up birds and other animals.

"Yuck. Who'd want a pet snake anyway?" asked Vanessa.

"I would!" replied Kyle. "But my folks won't let me have one. I wouldn't want a python though. It looks like they cause too many problems."

The Sleuths also learned about kudzu. This vine was brought over to the United States from Asia in the 1800s. It grows very fast, sometimes a foot a day!

"Boy, it sounds like the beanstalk from *Jack and the Beanstalk*," said Marco.

▼ **Kudzu**

"I remember seeing kudzu when we visited my aunt and uncle in Atlanta last year," Vanessa said. "It was growing all along the highway. It covered bushes, trees, walls, everything. It was weird."

Kyle shook his head. "Why would someone bring a vine over here?"

Jamie continued reading a magazine article about kudzu.

"It says here that the vine was used by farmers to control soil erosion. The government was very worried about erosion. In the 1930s and 40s, they paid farmers to plant kudzu."

"Well, it makes sense to try to prevent erosion," said Kyle, "but maybe they should've just planted grass."

The Sleuths continued to dig for more information on invaders.

"It's amazing how many plants and animals were brought to the United States from other countries," said Vanessa. "Look at this starling." She held open a book and pointed to a picture of a black bird with a short tail.

"I've seen that kind of bird," said Marco.

"Did you know they were brought over from Europe?" Vanessa asked. "Someone released a few in New York's Central Park over a hundred years ago. Now, they're all over the place. Sometimes they take over other birds' nests."

As the Sleuths did more research, they came to a conclusion—most plant and animal invaders do a lot of damage.

"It doesn't seem like people release invaders on purpose," said Jamie. "I mean, they don't mean to cause problems when they bring in these plants and animals."

Vanessa shook her head. "Yeah, but the problems still happen. Like with the zebra mussels. Who would have thought that these little critters would cause so many problems, like fewer fish, and bad-tasting water? I know the mussels were brought here by accident. But it still shows how one thing can lead to another."

"Well, I'm glad we'll be able to tell kids and adults about the zebra mussels," said Kyle. "Then they can help stop these invaders from spreading to new areas."

"You know," said Marco proudly, "I think this could be our most important article yet!"

Everyone agreed.

CASE CLOSED

How Is Water Cleaned?

Water in a river or stream may look clean, but it often has dirt and germs in it. So before water arrives at your home, it must get cleaned in a water treatment plant. Treatment plants make water safe for people to drink. Here's how it works.

Water First, a big pipe takes water from a source such as a lake. The water flows through the pipe into a treatment plant. Then the water gets dumped into large tanks.

▲ Water treatment plant

▲ Settling tanks

Chemicals In the tanks, chemicals are added to the water. The chemicals make bits of dirt clump together. The clumps sink to the bottom of the tank. They stay behind as the water flows out of the tank.

Filters Next, the water is passed through filters made of charcoal, sand, and gravel. These filters remove smaller pieces of dirt. The water is now free of dirt. But it might still have germs.

Filter ▶

Chlorine Finally, chlorine is added to the water. This chemical kills germs or other tiny living things still in the water. Now the water is safe for people to use. It is stored in a water tower or a reservoir until you turn on the tap. Then it flows through pipes to your home.

◀ Chlorine tanks

Be a Science Sleuth

The Science Sleuths used their questioning and research skills to solve a science mystery. Now you can be a sleuth, too.

- Copy the web below into your notebook.

- Choose a type of plant or animal invader and write it in the center oval.

- Fill in the rest of the ovals with questions you would like to research.

- Use books and the Internet to find answers to your questions.

- Write a three-paragraph essay explaining what you have learned from your research.

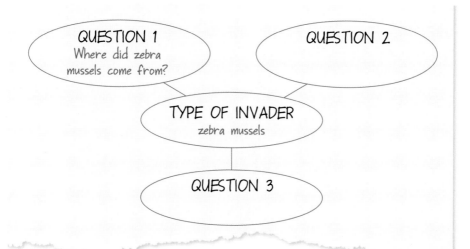

QUESTION 1
Where did zebra mussels come from?

QUESTION 2

TYPE OF INVADER
zebra mussels

QUESTION 3

Read More About Plant and Animal Invaders

Find and read more books about plant and animal invaders. As you read, think about these questions. They will help you understand more about this topic.

- What are the different types of plant and animal invaders where you live?

- What are some ways the invaders have affected the area where you live?

- How can you help stop the spread of the invaders in your area?

SUGGESTED READING
Reading Expeditions
Life Science:
Protecting the Planet